John Cousins   Patent It Yourself!

First published by BizB Press 2016

Copyright © 2016 by John J. Cousins

BizB supports copyright. Copyright fuels creativity, encourages diverse voices, promotes free speech, and creates vibrant culture. Thank you for buying an authorized edition of this book and for complying with copyright laws by not reproducing, scanning, or distributing any part of it in any form without permission. You are supporting writers and allowing BizB to continue to publish books for every reader.

ISBN 9781549517969

MBA ASAP

Patent It Yourself!

Turn your Ideas and Inventions into Valuable Intellectual Property

John Cousins

Sign up for my Newsletter and get free books. Sign up at www.mba-asap.com and receive **Reading and Understanding Financial Statements** absolutely free.

Receive announcements of free and discounted books and courses.

Dedicated to Thomas Edison and Nikola Tesla: Feuding geniuses and brilliant inventors.

Patent It Yourself!

Turn your ideas and inventions into valuable Intellectual Property

Contents

About the Author 9
Introduction 10
Disclaimer 11
Part I Overview ASAP 12
Outline of the Patent Application Process 12
    You only need two things: 12
    Application Process Steps 13
Why Patents Are Valuable 15
    The Patent Application Process is Also Valuable 19
    Thomas Edison Patent Master 22
    Word to the Wise: Don't Overspend 23
Part II Patent Law Rules and Regulations 23

Different Kinds of Intellectual Property 24
   Patents 25
   Monopoly 27
   There are Three Types of Patents: 28
      Utility 28
      Design 29
      Plant 30
   Provisional Patent Application 30
   Trademark and Servicemark 32
      Apple Corps vs. Apple Inc. 33
   Copyright 34
Patents and their Statutory Basis 36
Patents and the United States Constitution 37
Patent Laws 38
   U.S. Code: 35 USC 101 39
   America Invents Act (AIA) 41
      AIA Takeaway 42
      Other Intellectual Property Laws 43
   Trade Secrets 43
Where to File 46
   Functions of the United States Patent and Trademark Office 47

When to File 48
What Can Be Patented 48
Patentable Subject Matter 49
    Fields...49
    Limits on Subject Matter Eligibility 51
    Summary of Patent Eligibility 54
    Utility 55
Novelty and Non-Obviousness, Conditions for Obtaining A Patent 56
    Novelty 56
        Conditions for Patentability 57
    Prior Art 58
    Anticipation 60
    Non Obviousness 60
Effective Filing Date of the Claimed Invention 63
The Patent Application 63
Written Specifications and Claims 64
    35 U.S.C. 112..66
    Best Mode 69
Drawings...70
Inventorship 71
Filing Fees 72

File Assignments Before Paying Issue Fee 74
Part III Drafting and Filing Documents........................75
    Suggested Application Formatting Guidelines..........76
    Application Arrangement 77
    Title of the Invention 78
    Special Cases 79
Background of the Invention 80
    Field of Invention 80
    Description of the Related Art...................................80
Patent Related Art Reference Search Tips.....................81
    Search Keyword Development Methodology 82
    Evaluating the References 85
Summary of the Invention 85
    Brief Description of the Drawings............................87
    Detailed Description of the Invention.......................88
    Claims 89
    Drafting the Claims...89
    Abstract...91
    Patent Drawings..92
Sample Patent Application Template 93
Congratulations! It's Time to File 108

Patent Application Examination 108
    Examiner Process...109
    Amendment..111
    Issuance Fees 112
Summary...113

About the Author

John is an author of over 20 books, blogger, podcaster, online course creator, investor, inventor, entrepreneur and musician. John began his career, after graduating from Boston University and MIT with degrees in Media Studies and Electronics, working for one of the great early Silicon Valley tech firms: Ampex. He then spent a decade in Manhattan working for ABC Television as a systems engineer designing and building facilities for the network and managing programs for sports and news; big spectacles like the Olympics and political conventions.

John then received his MBA from Wharton. He has since taken two companies public as CFO and CEO and has had 15 years experience as a public company CFO and ten years experience as a public company CEO. John has been involved in many start up and public company financings and deal making. He has founded numerous startups in alternative energy, life sciences, and technology. His career shifted to teaching at numerous universities in the U.S. and internationally in the past ten years. His company MBA ASAP delivers digital content on business topics via eBooks, paperbacks, audiobooks, podcasts and online courses. Visit http://www.mba-asap.com/

Introduction

In the past decade the patent research, drafting, and filing process has evolved and the tools are now in place that make it feasible for you to perform all the steps and file your own patent.

The process hasn't gotten easier but the tools of word processing and the database on the United States Patent and Trademark Office website create an environment that empowers all of us to protect and commercialize our ideas and creativity.

This book looks at the patent application process from the standpoint of U.S. patent and filing procedures.

You can file your patent for under $500 and the average value of an issued patent is $1 million. This is lucrative work and well worth your time to learn.

Disclaimer

Information within this book does not constitute legal, financial or similar professional advice. The purchaser of this publication assumes full responsibility for the use of these materials and information. The Publisher and Author assume no liability whatsoever on behalf of any reader of this material. Please consult applicable laws and regulations and competent counsel to ensure your use of this material conforms with all applicable laws and regulations.

This is not legal advice and I do not promise that your patent will be awarded. That will rely on the strength of your invention and ability to adequately describe it and work with the patent office examiner. This book is a guide to that process.

Part I Overview ASAP

Outline of the Patent Application Process

Drafting a patent application is a surprisingly straightforward process. The hard part is having the idea of an invention. If you have ideas of things you think could be patented you owe it to yourself to read this book and draft an application. Even if you decide not to file it, this knowledge may come in handy for the next big idea you have. Then you will be ready to draft the application and won't be intimidated because you have done it already.

You only need two things:

- Access to a computer with a word processor. I use Microsoft Word. Apple also has a great word processor called Pages. And Google Docs is also a super (and free!) option.
- Access to the Internet so you can go to the U.S. Patent and Trademark Office (USPTO) website www.uspto.gov where you will perform your prior art search and research patented ideas similar to your invention. This is also where you electronically file your patent application.

Application Process Steps

Pro se is the legal term for representing yourself. You will be representing yourself to the USPTO and the patent examiner in the applications process. Here is an outline of the process so you can get an idea of the steps that will be outlined in more detail in this book:

- Come up with a title for your invention
- Write a short description of your invention.

- Use key words from you title and description as search terms in the database on the USPTO website. Copy the Abstract and patent number of patents and patent applications that are similar to yours.
- Write a description of why your patent is different from the similar ones already patented and published applications. This will become the Prior Art section of your application.
- Write a Summary of the Invention.
- Write a Brief Description of the Drawings. Every patent application needs to have at least one drawing that shows the parts of the invention.
- Write a Detailed Description of the Invention. This is where you discuss how to make and use the invention in as much detail as you can.
- Write the Claims. This is where you draft the different aspects of the invention each as a separate claim.
- Write the Abstract. This is a separate summary of the invention about one paragraph in length.

- Create the Drawings. You can do this in Word. It must be black and white and they are attached after the Abstract.

That's it! Those are the major sections of the application. When you have completed those parts to your satisfaction, you file it on the USPTO website along with a few short forms and your payment.

Then you wait six to twelve months to hear from your patent examiner who has reviewed your application. He or she will have questions regarding the prior art and your claims and you begin a process of responding to their questions. When they are answered satisfactorily, your patent will be ready to be awarded.

Why Patents Are Valuable

In most cases it only makes sense to patent ideas and inventions that you plan on commercializing. Patents are valuable because they represent a monopoly. You essentially get a 20-year monopoly on the business opportunity detailed by the invention. The patent represents competitive barriers to entry in the markets served.

Patents represent a strategic competitive advantage. In business, a competitive advantage is an attribute that allows an organization to outperform its competitors. A competitive advantage is what creates lasting value for a company.

Patents are a key piece of New Venture Strategy. Patents are strategically important, whether you are an entrepreneur with a start up idea, or working in an established company and have an idea that could expand a product or service line.

Once you have filed your patent, you have secured "patent pending" status.

"Patent pending" is a legal designation that can be used in relation to a product or process once a patent application for the product or process has been filed, but prior to the patent being issued or the application abandoned.

You can then feel free to talk about your invention with potential partners and investors because no one can steal your idea.

Patent pending represents an Asset that you can fund around. Investors like to fund assets. Filing a patent is a great strategy, and probably the least expensive way, to jump-start a venture.

An astute and experienced business mentor once advised me: "When in doubt, create assets." A patent application costs less than $500 to file and an issued patent is worth $1 million on average. That is tremendous value leverage. This can be the basis of creating significant personal wealth.

> When in doubt, create assets.

Once you learn and become familiar with this process, you can create a patent portfolio that could add significantly to your net worth. It is also tremendously satisfying to see your ideas transformed into valuable intellectual property.

Big companies are big players in intellectual property. Along with branding and Trademarks, patents are considered primary strategic assets. Over 200,000 patents are awarded annually in the U.S. The company that was awarded the most U.S. patents last year was Samsung with over 9,000!

Companies look to create monopolies through their patent portfolio. One patent does not a monopoly make. Astute entrepreneurs and corporate leaders pursue a strategy of developing multiple patents that surround a commercial venture's core ideas. This is called a Picket Fence Strategy.

Patents are the most liquid form of intellectual property, meaning they can be valued and sold. IBM sold a portfolio of more than 500 patents to Facebook and a portfolio of more than 900 patents to Twitter. Twitter paid $36 million for their portfolio.

The Patent Application Process is Also Valuable

The front-end process of drafting a patent application is valuable in and of itself because it will quickly flesh out if your idea is truly novel and what the competitive landscape surrounding it looks like. The patent application process is a disciplined methodology that rationalizes your idea or concept.

If you have an idea for a novel product or service, a patent application can be a great process to initially test that idea against what may already exist. The application process will answer several important initial questions.

First it helps to concretize your concept or idea. You have to think about the different attributes and write them down.

Second it forces you, in a disciplined manner, to articulate and define your value proposition and what is truly unique about it. The process of drafting the application clarifies one's ideas and value proposition.

This is a critical aspect of commercialization and will allow you to price your product or service at a premium.

Third the Prior Art search, conducted via key words in the search field of the USPTO database, forces you to examine similar patents and see what aspects of your concept or ideas represent something novel and unique. Searching, evaluating, and responding to prior art is a super methodology for competitive analysis. Your patent will act as a barrier to competitive entry into your market. This mitigates market risk and will make your enterprise more attractive to investors.

Fourth in a matter of hours you can assess whether you are really onto something or whether it has been thought of before. This is valuable to keep from wasting time.

Fifth drafting the application and filing it and receiving "patent pending" status lends credibility to you as a serious entrepreneur and businessperson. It creates a pre-money valuation for investment and licensing opportunities.

The application is a due diligence document that you can share, under a confidentiality agreement, with potential investors. It provides something concrete to analyze and their feedback and critiques can be very valuable. And they may fund your venture!

Sixth you can search and read all the patents in your field and get a sense of the competition.

You can search for Assignees and see what companies control what patents. The assignment of a patent is independent from the inventor. Patents are property. The assignee, usually a company, is the entity that has the property right to the patent. The inventor and the assignee may be the same, but an employee will assign a patent to the company they work for.

You can search on the Class and Subclass of your patent application to also uncover competitors. This is how patents are organized at the patent office. There are over 400 classes in the U.S. Patent Classification System. Each has a title descriptive of its subject matter is identified by a class number. Each class is subdivided into a number of subclasses with its own descriptive title and subclass number.

During the patent search process if you find relevant patents through your keyword search you can copy the classification number and search on that.

All of the information gathered from this process can be placed in your business plan and will make it a much more thorough and convincing document. This work creates clarity, reduces risk, and eliminates vagueness.

Patents create value, but only if they represent a commercially viable product or service. So don't think of a patent as a standalone entity but as an element in a strategic business context that you can execute on or license to someone else to bring to market.

Thomas Edison Patent Master

In the beginning of Edison's career he wrote all his own patents. In one year 1883 he drafted 106 patent applications that turned into patents. Thomas Edison was awarded 1093 patents issued in his name. That is the record!

Word to the Wise: Don't Overspend

There may be many things you can think of that can be patented. But be wise and frugal and only patent inventions that cover products you actually plan on selling.

If it doesn't have realistic markets and meet some customer need, then there is no commercial value and it may not be worth the cost and effort of patenting.

Part II Patent Law Rules and Regulations

This book primarily focuses on United States Patent Law and the Patent Application Process. International Patent Application Procedures for the Patent Cooperation Treaty (PCT) extends your United States Patent rights around the globe and will be discussed in further detail at the end of this book.

Different Kinds of Intellectual Property

There are four types of Intellectual Property protection of which patents are a subset. The four are:

- Patents
- Trademarks
- Servicemarks
- Copyrights

The rights that are protected under patents, copyrights, trademarks and servicemarks sometimes get confused and conflated. These are different kinds of intellectual property protection and they each serve different functions and purposes.

Trademarks and Servicemarks are similar but differ in that a trademark protects attributes of a product and a servicemark protects attributes of a service.

Copyright is a method of protection provided to the authors of "original works of authorship" including literary, dramatic, musical, and artistic.

I will go into more detail below on all four types of intellectual property protection starting with patents.

Patents

A patent is an exclusive property right for an invention and is granted to the inventor. The United States Patent and Trademark Office issue patents. The term length of a new patent is 20 years from the date on which the application for the patent was filed in the United States. This property right is subject to the payment of application, grant, and maintenance fees. U.S. patent grants are effective only within the United States, U.S. territories, and U.S. possessions.

The right conferred by the patent grant is: "the right to exclude others from making, using, offering for sale, or selling" the invention in the United States or "importing" the invention into the United States.

What is granted is not the right to make, use, offer for sale, sell or import, but the right to *exclude others* from making, using, offering for sale, selling or importing the invention. Once a patent is issued, the holder of the patent must enforce the patent through the courts if there is infringement.

Your patent gives you rights to enforce the patent against infringers but it requires having serious money in the bank to pursue enforcement through litigation. It is not automatic. If a cease and desist letter doesn't stop the infringement, a lawsuit can easily run into the millions of dollars. Check with your attorney if you discover potential infringement on your patent.

International patent rights can be applied for and granted based on an underlying U.S. patent application.

Monopoly

Economists use two terms to describe the nature of competition in markets: perfect competition and monopoly. Perfect competition is where you have lots of alternative products to choose from and they can only really compete on price. In this case profits have been squeezed to zero. This is not a good place to be in business. Monopoly on the other hand is where there is no competition and the seller can command a premium profit for the product. This is where you want to be positioned. You want to own the market and set your price. Competition is for losers.

This is what makes patents so valuable. A patent essentially gives you a legal monopoly to make, use and sell your invention. You get this legally protected monopoly status for twenty years from the application date. After that time, the invention goes into the public domain. An example of this process is when the patent on a pharmaceutical expires and then generic versions of the drug appear on the market.

There are Three Types of Patents:

Utility

Utility patents are what we will be focusing on in this book. Utility Patents cover the embodiment of an invention. The embodiment appears in the description of patent applications and is the term used to introduce a particular implementation or method of carrying out the invention.

Utility patents are granted to anyone who invents or discovers anything new and useful. A utility patent usually relates to a process, or a machine, but it can also be an article of manufacture, a composition of matter (like a new chemical compound), or any new and useful improvement to something previously existing in these categories.

Utility patents are the most commonly applied for.

Design

A "utility patent" protects the way an article is used and works, while a "design patent" protects the way an article looks. The ornamental appearance for an article includes its shape/configuration or surface ornamentation applied to the article, or both.

Patents may be granted to anyone who invents a new, original, and ornamental design for an article of manufacture. If you are a graphic or industrial designer or an architect, this category may be for you. This category is important to businesses in order to cover the design of their products, things like the tread design on tires or the shape of a bottle.

Design patents are for the cosmetic look only, not for its use. This can be a common confusion. If you intend to protect how something works, it's a utility patent you want to file. The design of a coke bottle is an example of a successful design patent.

Plant

Patents may be granted to anyone who invents or discovers and asexually reproduces any distinct and new variety of plant. There are many patents in seeds that produce more agricultural yield.

Provisional Patent Application

There is a type of preliminary Utility patent application called a **Provisional** application.

Provisional patent only applies to an application process. There is no such thing as a provisional patent. A provisional patent application requires follow-up with a full-fledged utility patent application. This must occur within one year. It is only possible to file a Provisional Patent Application for utility patents.

Why file the provisional if you need to file a regular utility patent application anyway? Good question. A provisional patent application is quick and less expensive to prepare.

It can speed up the first to file advantage by providing an early effective filing date. The primary benefit is the time prioritizing of one's claim relative to the claims of others.

But you run the risk of not filing the utility follow-up on time. And after one year your invention goes into the public domain and you have lost out. Also the clock starts ticking on your potential patent term. The term of a patent is **20 years** from the earliest filing date of the application. If you chew up a year on the front end with a provisional, which reduces your useable patent term.

Provisional applications are not examined. In contrast to the regular application, the provisional format has less formal requirements. A provisional application doens't required formal patent claims, an oath or declaration. Provisional applications also should not include any prior art disclosure.

It does allow you to use the term "Patent Pending" on the invention.

After filing a provisional, you must file a non-provisional within 1 year.

The non-provisional application is more detailed. But the discipline of the process ensures your invention meets the approval criteria.

Think hard about filing a provisional application. It rarely makes sense. It is my opinion that provisionals are not worth filing. It creates more work and extra costs.

Don't bother getting caught up in the extra step and expense of filing a provisional; go for the gusto!

Trademark and Servicemark

Trademarks and Servicemarks are similar. The difference between the two is that a trademark protects attributes of a product and a servicemark protects attributes of a service. Trademarks and service marks that are used in interstate or foreign commerce should be registered with the USPTO. This registration is used to protect the branding of products and services like brand names and logos.

A trademark is a word, name, symbol, or device that is used in trade with goods to indicate the source of the goods and to distinguish them from the goods of others. A servicemark is the same as a trademark except that it identifies and distinguishes the source of a service rather than a product. The terms "trademark" and "mark" are commonly used to refer to both trademarks and servicemarks.

Trademark rights may be used to prevent others from using a confusingly similar mark, but not to prevent others from making the same goods or from selling the same goods or services under a clearly different mark.

The registration procedure for trademarks and general information concerning trademarks can be found on the USPTO website under the section entitled "Basic Facts about Trademarks." Here is a link to that webpage. (http://www.uspto.gov/trademarks/basics/Basic_Facts_Trademarks.jsp).

Here is an example of a famous trademark dispute.

Apple Corps vs. Apple Inc.

The right to trademark the word "apple" has been

contentious. The Beatles music company Apple Corps was first. Eight years later Steve Jobs created Apple Inc. Over the years, the two corporations have battled it out in lengthy litigation.

In the first round, Apple Inc. agreed to pay Apple Corps a cash settlement and stay out of the music business. But with the advent of iTunes, the legal wrangling again heated up.

They reached a settlement after Apple Inc. agreed to buy Apple Corps' trademark rights and then license them back to the music company.

That's a lot of legal fees over a piece of fruit.

Copyright

Copyright is a method of protection provided to the authors of "original works of authorship" including literary, dramatic, musical, artistic, and certain other intellectual works, both published and unpublished.

The copyright protects the form of expression rather than the subject matter of the writing.

The Copyright Act of 1976 gives the owner of copyright the exclusive right to reproduce the copyrighted work, to distribute copies or recordings of the copyrighted work, to perform the copyrighted work publicly, or to display the copyrighted work publicly.

The Copyright Office of the Library of Congress registers copyrights.

Copyrights are big business in the music industry. Publishing income comes from ownership of the copyrights in the songs, not the sound recordings. Songwriters typically own the copyrights in the music and lyrics to the songs they write. They earn money from license fees and royalties from the commercial use of their songs.

There are also publishing companies that purchase the copyrights of songs. Michael Jackson bought the Beatles song catalog. ATV acquired Northern Songs, publisher of the Lennon–McCartney song catalogue, in 1969. Michael Jackson purchased ATV Music in 1985 for

$47.5 million. Every time you hear a Beatles song on the radio, Michael's estate gets paid.

Signing away their publishing rights for small compensation in contracts with producers and record companies has ripped off many music artists in the past.

Owners of music copyrights guard their rights and are always on the lookout for hit songs that copy their melody. They sue if they hear something they think is too close to their song. There is a saying in the music business: "If you have a hit, you will get a writ."

Patents and their Statutory Basis

One of the basic rules of law in the United States is the legal protection of private property. Inventions are considered intellectual property and ownership of that property is protected under patents and patent law.

The legal basis of patent protection starts with the founding document of the United States: the U.S. Constitution. It travels through a number of more granular and detailed documents covering all the specifics. This chain is called the Statutory Basis and goes as follows:

- U.S. Constitution; Article 1, Section 8, Clause 8
- U.S. Code: 35 USC 101
- Government Code of Regulation: CFR 37
- Manual of Patent Examining Procedure (MPEP)
- Case Law

Below is a little more detail on the Statutory Basis. This information will be helpful when the patent examiner provides a response to you patent application. The examiner will refer to these laws.

Patents and the United States Constitution

Property rights are protected under the US Constitution. Patents are protected as Intellectual Property.

The Constitution of the United States provides Congress with the power to enact laws relating to patents, in Article I, section 8, clause 8 which states "Congress shall have power . . . to promote the progress of science and useful arts, by securing for limited times to authors and inventors the exclusive right to their respective writings and discoveries."

This is the authority from which the patent laws in the U.S. Code derive.

Patent Laws

The patent law specifies the subject matter for which a patent may be obtained and the conditions for patentability. We will discuss these in detail and clarify how to research, draft and file your patent. Don't be intimidated by the language and comprehensive nature of the patent law. It is drafted to protect your rights. Here is a short history and summary of the patent law so you can understand its context and navigate it when needed.

Under this power Congress has enacted various laws from time to time relating to patents. The first patent law was enacted in 1790.

U.S. Code: 35 USC 101

To address modern technology and inventions, the patent laws underwent a general revision in the early 1950s. It is codified in Title 35, United States Code.

Title 35 of the United States Code is the title of U. S. Code relating to patent law. The sections of Title 35 govern all aspects of patent law in the United States. I will refer to the sections so that you can access and read the actual law when you have specific questions.

The law refers to all kinds of specific situations and is very complete. Most of it will not apply to your specific case so don't be intimidated by its comprehensive nature.

Just know that you can refer to it when you need it and that you will know what patent attorneys, agents, and examiners are talking about when they refer to it.

This is especially important relative to patent examiners because they will reference the specific sections in their response letter to your application. That is when you will want to review those sections if there is an issue that they raise. There are currently 37 chapters, which include 376 sections in Title 35. There are a handful that are generally most useful in crafting and drafting your application.

Title 35 is grouped in four parts:

- Part I—United States Patent and Trademark Office
- Part II—Patentability of Inventions and Grant of Patents
- Part III—Patents and Protection of Patent Rights
- Part IV—Patent Cooperation Treaty

We will be most interested in Part II, which outlines and details what is patentable and how patents are granted.

Part IV covers international patent rights. We will discuss those also.

America Invents Act (AIA)

The America Invents Act (AIA) is a United States federal statute that was passed by Congress and was signed into law by President Barack Obama on September 16, 2011. The law represents the most significant change to the U.S. patent system since Title 35 was adopted in the 1950s.

The most significant change is that the Act changes the U.S. patent system from a "first to invent" to a "first inventor to file" system. First inventor to file is the way the rest of the world operates its patent laws so now the U.S. is "harmonized" with other countries. The central provisions of AIA went into effect on September 16, 2012 and on March 16, 2013.

Besides switching the U.S. patent rights from the previous "first-to-invent" system to a "first inventor-to-file" system, the law also expanded the definition of prior art used in determining patentability. Prior art is the term used to judge whether the proposed invention was known to the public prior to the patent application. If the invention is judged to have been publicly disclosed before you file for your patent, it is deemed ineligible.

Actions and prior art that bar patentability under the Act include public use, sales, publications, and other disclosures available to the public anywhere in the world as of the filing date. The law also expands prior art to include foreign offers for sale and public uses.

AIA Takeaway

So don't disclose your invention before you file your patent application and file ASAP. Don't write about it in an article or research paper or talk about it in a speech or offer it for sale before you file.

You only need a conceptual reduction to practice in order to file. This means you don't need a working model or prototype. If you can reduce your concept to practice in detailed sequential steps, the time to file is now!

Other Intellectual Property Laws

Other federally recognized forms of intellectual property are distributed throughout the United States Code. Copyrights are covered under Title 17. Trademark and unfair competition law is defined in Chapter 22 of Title 15 and Trade Secrets law, another form of intellectual property, is defined in Title 18 of the U.S.C.

Trade Secrets

There are two ways to protect an innovation. You can choose to patent it or keep it secret. We have been discussing at length the benefits of patents. Some perceived advantages of trade secrets are:

- Trade secrets can protect "abstract ideas" and patents cannot.
- The protection under trade secret remains for an unlimited period of time.
- There are no filing fees for trade secret protection.
- A trade secret creates cache and an aura of mystery.

Trade secrets are proprietary information that is not publicly disclosed. Trade secrets require agreement between parties not to disclose and are covered under Confidentiality and Non-disclosure agreements between the parties.

An example of a trade secret is the formula for making Coca Cola.

One of the most famous American trade secrets is the recipe for Coca-Cola. The mystique surrounding the formula has lasted more than 100 years. It has been the source of publicity and marketing campaigns. It has also been an enduring intellectual property protection strategy.

In 1886, Dr. John Pemberton created the Coca-Cola formula. Caffeine and sugar are ingredients. Other ingredients have been the source of speculation. One ingredient is the legendary "merchandise 7X". What the "X" factor is in the original formula has never been revealed. It may contain essential citrus oils of orange, lemon, and lime. Lavender may be another ingredient.

Only a small group of executives know the entire formula. No contractor has the complete recipe and each only makes a part of the famous blend.

The formula would have long since entered the public domain had the company patented it. They would have had only twenty years of exclusive rights to their classic blend.

The trade secret approach locks it up forever, as long as the secret is well kept.

There is risk of disclosure. It is not illegal to reverse engineer and copy a trade secret. Patent protection lasts 20 years and is more secure. In a patent lawsuit, independent invention is not a defense.

It depends on the nature of the innovation. You may want to discuss it with potential partners and investors. It may be easy to reverse engineer. In these cases file a patent before disclosing it. If it is a secret recipe like Dr. Pepper or Colonel Sander's KFC spices, then a trade secret works well.

Where to File

The United States Patent and Trademark Office (USPTO) is responsible for granting and issuing patents and registering trademarks. Part I of Title 35 establishes the scope, tasks and responsibilities of the USPTO.

When you have completed application, you file it electronically with the United States Patent and Trademark Office (USPTO). You file through their website www.uspto.gov. This is the same website that houses the database you will search as part of drafting the prior art section of your application. The United States Patent and Trademark Office is responsible for administering the law relating to the granting of patents.

Functions of the United States Patent and Trademark Office

The USPTO is an agency of the U.S. Department of Commerce. The role of the USPTO is to grant patents for the protection of inventions and to register trademarks. It serves the interests of inventors and businesses with respect to their inventions, products and services.

Through the preservation, classification, and dissemination of patent information, the USPTO's mandate is to help promote the industrial and technological progress of the Untied States and strengthen the economy through fostering innovation.

As part of its patent related duties, the USPTO examines applications and grants patents on inventions when applicants are entitled to them. It also publishes and disseminates patent information, records assignments of patents, maintains search files of U.S. and foreign patents, and maintains a searchable database for public use in examining issued patents and published patent applications.

The USPTO has an important strategic mission related to protecting intellectual endeavors and encouraging technological progress. The USPTO seeks to preserve and promote the United States' technological edge, which is key to its future competitiveness and prosperity.

When to File

Recall that U.S. patent law, under AIA, is now "first to file". File as soon as you have your conception and can write a description of how to make and use it. You must disclose the best mode, the best embodiment of the invention and you must have claims drafted. You can be a big winner if you file ASAP!

What Can Be Patented

There are four general categories of criteria that must be met in order to be granted a patent:

- Eligibility: the invention must fall into one or more of four fields of subject matter
- Utility: it must be specifically and substantially useful
- Novelty: it must be distinguished from prior patents and public information
- Non obviousness: it must not be an obvious combination of prior patents and public information

Patentable Subject Matter

Patent law specifies the fields of subject matter that can be patented and the conditions under which a patent may be obtained.

Fields

35 USC 101 is the section of the patent law that details what kinds of inventions are patentable.

It states that anyone who "invents or discovers any new and useful process, machine, manufacture, or composition of matter, or any new and useful improvement thereof, may obtain a patent".

There are four basic kinds of inventions that are patentable:

Process is defined by patent law as a process, act, or method, and primarily includes industrial or technical processes. Claims that you write about your invention in this category are usually referred to as "process" or "method" claims.

Machine refers to the parts that functionally interact to make the invented process happen. In most cases they are moving parts but they can also be parts that interact functionally in an electronic circuit for example. The claims that you write about your invention in this category are referred to as "machine" claims. A standard patent application may have a number of process claims and a number of machine claims.

Manufacture refers to articles that are made and this category includes all manufactured articles.

Composition of matter relates to chemical compositions and may include mixtures of ingredients as well as new chemical compounds. These classes of subject matter taken together cover most everything that is made by man and the processes for making them.

Limits on Subject Matter Eligibility

These fields of subject matter are quite wide ranging and expansive but there are certain areas and subject matter that have been deemed ineligible. These are called 101 judicial exceptions because they have been circumscribed by court decisions and are part of the case law related to patents. [1]

The below is a quotation from the Manual of Patent Examining Procedure (MPEP) relating to ineligibility. It

---

[1] The Supreme Court of the United States in a decision Bilski v. Kappos interpreted 35 USC 101.

includes citations of the court cases that defined the status. [2]

706.03(a) Rejections Under 35 U.S.C. 101

I. SUBJECT MATTER ELIGIBILITY

Patents are not granted for all new and useful inventions and discoveries. The subject matter of the invention or discovery must come within the boundaries set forth by 35 U.S.C. 101, which permits patents to be granted only for "any new and useful process, machine, manufacture, or composition of matter, or any new and useful improvement thereof."

The term "process" as defined in 35 U.S.C. 100, means process, art or method, and includes a new use of a known process, machine, manufacture, composition of matter, or material.

Judicial court decisions have determined the limits of the statutory classes. Examples of subject matter not patentable under the statute follow:

---

[2] This is taken from 8th Ed. Revision 6, Sept 2007.

A. Printed Matter

For example, a mere arrangement of printed matter, though seemingly a "manufacture," is rejected as not being within the statutory classes. See In re Miller, 418 F.2d 1392, 164 USPQ 46 (CCPA 1969); Ex parte Gwinn, 112 USPQ 439 (Bd. App. 1955); and In re Jones, 373 F.2d 1007, 153 USPQ 77 (CCPA 1967).

B. Naturally Occurring Article

Similarly, a thing occurring in nature, which is substantially unaltered, is not a "manufacture." A shrimp with the head and digestive tract removed is an example. Ex parte Grayson, 51 USPQ 413 (Bd. App. 1941).

C. Scientific Principle

A scientific principle, divorced from any tangible structure, can be rejected as not within the statutory classes. O"Reilly v. Morse, 56 U.S. (15 How.) 62 (1854).

This subject matter is further limited by the Atomic Energy Act explained in MPEP § 706.03(b).

Don't get too hung up on the technical legal jargon here. I shared this so you know there are limits to what is patentable and these limits have been set by court decisions.

Summary of Patent Eligibility

Remember, whoever invents or discovers any **new** and **useful**

- Process
- Machine
- Manufacture
- Composition of matter
- Or any **new** and **useful** improvement thereof,

can obtain a patent on it.

Notice that I put **New** and **Useful** in bold. Patents are subject to the conditions and requirements of the patent law. These require that a patent be novel and have utility. We will discuss these conditions and requirements next.

Utility

The patent law specifies that the subject matter must be "useful." The term "useful" in this context refers to the condition that the subject matter has a useful purpose and also includes operativeness. This means a machine invention must operate to perform the intended purpose or it would not be called useful, and therefore would not be granted a patent.

The courts have interpreted the patent statute over time and have defined the limits of the field of subject matter that can be patented. The laws of nature, physical phenomena, and abstract ideas are not patentable subject matter.

A patent cannot be obtained upon a mere idea or suggestion. It must have a tangible embodiment that is detailed in the description, claims and drawings. The patent is granted upon the new process, machine, manufacture, etc. and a complete description of the actual machine or other subject matter for which a patent is sought is required.

Novelty and Non-Obviousness, Conditions for Obtaining A Patent

Novelty

In order for an invention to be patentable it must be distinguished from the prior art and deemed "new" as defined in the patent law. An invention cannot be patented if:

"(1) the claimed invention was patented, described in a printed publication, or in public use, on sale, or otherwise available to the public before the effective filing date of the claimed invention" or

"(2) the claimed invention was described in a patent issued [by the U.S.] or in an application for patent published or deemed published [by the U.S.], in which the patent or application, as the case may be, names another inventor and was effectively filed before the effective filing date of the claimed invention."

In patent prohibition (1), the term "otherwise available to the public" refers to other types of disclosures of the claimed invention such as, an oral presentation at a scientific meeting, a demonstration at a trade show, a lecture or speech, a research paper, a statement made on a radio talk show, a YouTube video, or a website or other on-line material.

You also cannot get a patent on a new use or benefit related to an old and already patented or disclosed device.

Conditions for Patentability

35 U.S.C. 102 is entitled "Conditions for Patentability". This section describes some of the conditions for when a patent should not be granted to an inventor based on the concept of novelty. These conditions generally relate to

when an invention is already known publicly. The term for something already known publicly if "prior art" and refers to previously issued patents and applications, and things that have been publicly disclosed.

Prior Art

Prior Art is the term used to describe previous inventions that are patented or disclosed publicly. It is your responsibility to make a search of previous inventions and make sure that your invention is actually new and unique and hasn't been detailed and described before. Luckily the research process has been greatly simplified by the introduction of the searchable database on the USPTO website.

The various subsections of 35 U.S.C. 102 describe different kinds of prior art that can provide evidence that a proposed invention has already been made public, including inventions that have already been patented or described in other patent applications or publications.

Section 102 also includes inventions that have been on sale for more than a year before the patent application was filed. The case law provided by the ruling in Netscape Communications Corp. v. Konrad focuses on the public use and on-sale criteria of section 102.

35 U.S.C. 102 was revised by the America Invents Act (AIA). The most important part of section 102, which was also referenced above, now reads as follows:

(a) NOVELTY; PRIOR ART.—A person shall be entitled to a patent unless—

(1) the claimed invention was patented, described in a printed publication, or in public use, on sale, or otherwise available to the public before the effective filing date of the claimed invention; or

(2) the claimed invention was described in a patent issued under section 151, or in an application for patent published or deemed published under section 122(b), in which the patent or application, as the case may be, names another inventor and was effectively filed before the effective filing date of the claimed invention.

The full text can be found at the USPTO website.

Anticipation

Another concept detailed in 35 USC 102 is Anticipation. Anticipation is related to the concept of Novelty: a proposed invention must be novel or not anticipated by a single prior art reference.

In the Prior Art section of your application you will list similar patents and patent application that you found searching the USPTO database. In Part II of this book we will go through a sample patent application template that will make this process clear.

Non Obviousness

35 U.S.C. 103 describes the condition of patentability known as non-obviousness. This section states that a patentable invention must not have been obvious to a "person having ordinary skill in the art" in view of the appropriate prior art.

A patent may be refused if the differences between your invention and other existing patents are considered so slight as to be obvious. Even if the invention proposed to be patented is not exactly shown by the prior art, and involves incremental differences to subject matter already known and considered too similar, a patent may still be refused. The differences must not be considered to be obvious.

The invention presented to be patented must be sufficiently different from what has been used or described before that it is considered by the patent examiner to be non-obvious to a person having ordinary skill in the area of technology related to the invention. This is the test that examiners use for non obviousness. For example, superficial changes like changing one color for another, or changes in size, are not patentable.

There has to be some meaningful inventiveness going on in what you are claiming is your invention. In European patent law they use the expression "inventive step", while the term "non-obviousness" is used in United States patent law although the term "inventiveness" is sometimes used as well in the U.S. These terms can be considered synonyms as the basic principle is roughly the same.

The inventive step and non-obviousness represent a general patentability requirement. An invention should be sufficiently inventive—i.e., non-obvious—in order to be patented. The criteria you must meet is whether the invention is an adequate distance beyond or above the existing state of the art.

Section 103 was also revised by AIA and now reads:

A patent for a claimed invention may not be obtained, notwithstanding that the claimed invention is not identically disclosed as set forth in section 102, if the differences between the claimed invention and the prior art are such that the claimed invention as a whole would have been obvious before the effective filing date of the claimed invention to a person having ordinary skill in the art to which the claimed invention pertains. Patentability shall not be negated by the manner in which the invention was made.

The full text of this section of the statute can be found at the USPTO website.

Effective Filing Date of the Claimed Invention

The term "effective filing date of the claimed invention" means the actual filing date of the U.S. nonprovisional patent application. This is the date that starts the clock ticking on your patent's life.

The Patent Application

35 USC Section 111 details the content of the patent application for both provisional and non-provisional applications. Since we are not interested in ever filing a provisional application (see the section above "Never bother filing a provisional application") we will look at what is required as content in the non-provisional application.

Here is a list of the contents of the Patent Application:

- You must include written specifications drafted as per 35 USC 112
- You must include at least one drawing as per 35 USC 113

    – Black and White; 1" margins; number coordinated with the Description

    – You must have a drawing

- You must include an oath by the applicant as per 35 USC 115. This is where you declare that you are the inventor of the invention claimed in the application. Make sure all joint inventors are acknowledged and execute an oath or declaration in connection with the application.

- You must pay the fees required by law. As an individual you most likely will qualify to pay the Micro Entity fees and I will detail those for you. Micro entity is a discount on fees for small businesses that meet the requirements. The fees change from time to time and you should check the USPTO website before filing.

Written Specifications and Claims

The main part of your patent application is the written description of the invention and the Claims section where you detail each aspect of the invention separately. The level of detail varies in the written description section based on the nature and scope of the claims and the complexity of the relevant technology.

In the description and claims you are not describing the function of your invention or the end result of what it does. You are writing out the concrete steps of how it works. Your job is to sufficiently identify and describe <u>how</u> the claimed function is achieved.

You specification and description should teach someone how to make the invention. This is called the Enablement. You task is to bridge the gap between someone knowledgeable in the field and art and your invention.

You are also required to identify and state the Best Mode for making your invention. There may be several ways to make it and you need to state which you feel is the best way. Use the term "Best Mode" when identifying it as this is a specific patent requirement.

35 U.S.C. 112

35 U.S.C. 112 details the requirements regarding the form and content of the specification and the claims. The first paragraph (a) introduces 3 legal concepts, the written description requirement, the enablement requirement, and the best mode requirement. The second paragraph (b) limits the ability of claims to be too open-ended or unclear.

Post-AIA section 112 reads as follows:

35 U.S.C. 112 Specification.

(a) IN GENERAL. —The specification shall contain a written description of the invention, and of the manner and process of making and using it, in such full, clear, concise, and exact terms as to enable any person skilled in the art to which it pertains, or with which it is most nearly connected, to make and use the same, and shall set forth the best mode contemplated by the inventor or joint inventor of carrying out the invention.

(b) CONCLUSION.—The specification shall conclude with one or more claims particularly pointing out and distinctly claiming the subject matter which the inventor or a joint inventor regards as the invention.

(c) FORM.—A claim may be written in independent or, if the nature of the case admits, in dependent or multiple dependent form.

(d) REFERENCE IN DEPENDENT FORMS.—Subject to subsection (e), a claim in dependent form shall contain a reference to a claim previously set forth and then specify a further limitation of the subject matter claimed. A claim in dependent form shall be construed to incorporate by reference all the limitations of the claim to which it refers.

(e) REFERENCE IN MULTIPLE DEPENDENT FORM.—A claim in multiple dependent form shall contain a reference, in the alternative only, to more than one claim previously set forth and then specify a further limitation of the subject matter claimed. A multiple dependent claim shall not serve as a basis for any other multiple dependent claim. A multiple dependent claim shall be construed to incorporate by reference all the limitations of the particular claim in relation to which it is being considered.

(f) ELEMENT IN CLAIM FOR A COMBINATION.—An element in a claim for a combination may be expressed as a means or step for performing a specified function without the recital of structure, material, or acts in support thereof, and such claim shall be construed to cover the corresponding structure, material, or acts described in the specification and equivalents thereof.

This specification 112 is the core of the patent application and that is why I have included it here for reference. Don't get intimidated by the legalese style of the language. In summary it requires that:

- The Specification shall be complete

- With enough information to enable one of ordinary skill in that art to make and use the invention

- Shall set for the **best mode** contemplated by the inventor for carrying out the invention.

- The specification shall conclude with one of more claims. These can be both independent and dependant claims.

I will go into more detail on these points so don't be concerned if they are not completely clear to you at this point. Stay calm; you can do this.

Best Mode

This is important. In your Detailed Description of the Invention section you must describe in detail the Best Mode of the invention. This means the optimal way you conceive of implementing the invention. Best Mode is required by 35 USC 112, which states:

Specification shall be complete enough to enable one of ordinary skill in that art to make and use the invention and shall set forth the best mode contemplated by the inventor for carrying out the invention.

Not including a clear description of the Best Mode of embodying the invention will leave your patent vulnerable to infringement should you ever contest it in court. Include it.

Drawings

As per 35 USC 113, drawings shall be included where needed to understand the invention. Drawings must be Black and White unless a petition to the USPTO is granted as to why shaded or color is required in order to properly describe the invention.

The drawing must have 1" margins on all four sides.

You must label various details in the drawings and describe the labels in the written section called Description of Drawings.

Microsoft Word has adequate drawing tools and capabilities to handle most drawing needs.

You must include a drawing. At least one drawing is required for any patent application.

Inventorship

As per 35 USC 115, an application for patent needs to include the name of the inventor for any part of the invention claimed in the application. Each individual who is the inventor, or a joint inventor, of the claimed invention needs to execute an oath or declaration to that effect in the application.

This is where you sign an oath that you are in fact the inventor. This is important. Signing a declaration knowing that you have not named inventorship in accordance with the Patent Act is a Federal Crime under 18 USC 1001.

Filing Fees

There are three pricing tiers for patents: Full Fee, Small Entity and Micro Entity. Micro Entity is the one we will be most interested in as first time filers.

The AIA revisions to the patent laws added the micro-entity status. A micro-entity includes an independent inventor with a gross income of less than 3 times the national median household income. You also can't have previously filed more than four non-provisional patent applications.

The Full fee for filing a non-provisional utility patent application is $1600. The Small Entity fee is 50% of the Full fee or $800. The Micro Entity fee is 50% of the Small Entity Fee or $400.

So a micro-entity is entitled to a 75% reduction in many of the patent fees payable to the US Patent Office during the prosecution of a US patent application.

To be eligible for Micro Entity status you must meet these criteria:

- Applicant or any inventor must not have filed more than 4 non-provisional patent applications
- Must not have made more than approximately $160,000 in income in last year

If you are in the enviable position of not meeting these criteria, you should find the small entity fee schedule also very reasonable.

Here is a detailed list of the Micro Entity fees:

- E-File Filing Fee $70
- Search Fee $150
- Examination $180
- Add those up for a Total E-Filing of $400

The total filing fee is $400. When you have your patent granted there will be two additional fees:

- Issue Fee $240

- Publication Fee $300

Remember these fees are subject to change so always check the fee schedule posted on the USPTO website before filing.

File Assignments Before Paying Issue Fee

The assignment is where you assign your patent to a company. As a commercial venture you will initially apply for the patent as the inventor and when it gets awarded, assign it to your company.

Patent Rule 37 CFR 3.81 requires that assignments be recorded (filed with the patent office) before the issue fee is paid. The assignment must be made before the patent office will issue patent to the assignee or recognize assignee on the issued patent. So if you are planning on assigning your patent to a company or enterprise you control, this is the time to make the assignment.

It is a good idea to wait on assigning the patent until it has been approved so that you can discuss any issues that arise with the patent examiner as the inventor. It is much better to discuss any concerns the examiner has directly as the inventor. The examiner can be very helpful in guiding an inventor in the process.

Part III Drafting and Filing Documents

Title 37 of the Code of Federal Regulations (CFR) details the rules for corresponding with the USPTO. We will go through the rules for our patent application. This includes the parts and information the application must contain. I also go over the structure and formatting of the application. After I discuss each individual part, I will provide a sample application template so you can see how all the parts fit together and their sequence.

Suggested Application Formatting Guidelines

Here is a summary to follow for the application format:

- File electronically
- 1" margins all around text and drawings
- 12 point font
- Arial, Times Roman or Courier
- Double space all text
- All paragraphs should be serially numbered [0001]
- Claims must start on a new page and each Claim separately numbered starting with Claim 1
- The pages of the Application including the Claims must be numbered consecutively, starting with 1, the numbers being centrally located preferably below the text.
- Abstract must start on a new page with NO page number

I include a sample application template later in this book that follows these formatting guidelines and will help you better understand with a detailed example.

Application Arrangement

37 CFR 1.77 details the arrangement and sequencing of the various patent application sections. Here they are:

- Title of the Invention (maximum 500 characters – less is better)
- Cross reference to related applications (if applicable)
- Statement regarding federally sponsored R&D (if applicable)
- Names of Parties to a joint research agreement (if applicable)
- Statement regarding prior disclosures
- Background of the Invention

- Field of Invention
- Description of the Related Art
- Brief Summary of the Invention
- Brief Description of the Drawings
- Detailed Description of the Invention
- Claims (start on a new page)
- Abstract of the Disclosure (start on a new page, single paragraph of 150 words or less)
- Drawings (start on a new page)
- Executed Oath of Declaration

I will now go through each of these in some detail to give you an idea of what is required. Then we will move on to a sample application template and put it all together. After that you will be ready to draft and file your first patent!

Title of the Invention

37 CFR 1.72 details the requirement of the Title of your invention. The title of the invention may not exceed 500 characters in length and must be as short and specific as possible.

International patent rights are guided by the Patent Cooperation Treaty (PCT). The PCT requires that the Title should fairly describe the scope of the disclosure in **6 words or less.** So it is best to adhere to this restriction and keep your Title to six words or less.

Special Cases

Cross reference to related applications including like a statement regarding federally sponsored R&D, names of parties to a joint research agreement, statement regarding prior disclosures, are applicable only in special cases so I won't go into detail on these. The forms are fairly self-explanatory. Fill them out and include them if you fall into any of these categories.

Background of the Invention

This section includes the Field of the Invention and Description of the Related Art.

Field of Invention

Write one **short** paragraph stating the technical field of the invention so that the USPTO examiners may properly classify the application and route it to an examiner with that expertise.

This paragraph can be very similar the Abstract which comes at the end of the application. You can essentially reproduce the Abstract here as the Field of Invention.

Description of the Related Art

Include approximately 3 to 6 existing patents and/or published applications that are related in subject matter or are analogous in some way. This is also referred to as "prior art". You can find the prior art at www.uspto.gov website. There is a searchable database of all patents and applications and you can search using keywords that describe your invention.

Read the Titles and Abstracts of patents that seem similar and choose the ones that contain similarities. Reference them by patent number and copy and paste the Abstract. Conclude with statement about why it is deficient compared to your invention.

Don't use Google or other search engines to search for prior art because they sell searches and companies and individuals looking for good ideas to patent purchase those search results. Remember its a first to file world.

Patent Related Art Reference Search Tips

In the Related Art section of your patent application you want to reference a number of patents and patent applications that discuss similar inventions. The goal here is to search the USPTO database and disclose similar inventions and discuss why they are not identical to yours. This is where you make you case that your invention is new and unique and has not been previously patented or disclosed.

The USPTO database is searchable in a similar fashion to how you use Google's search engine. It relies on key words. This searchable database is a powerful tool that has made writing your own patent application a viable proposition. It has only been available for the last 15 years or so. Before that you had to hire a law firm in Washington to physically go through the patent books and research and locate the pertinent analogous patents. This was an expensive undertaking that limited the general public's ability to research and report on the prior art.

Search Keyword Development Methodology

Let's talk about a methodology for developing and refining your key word search. Its an iterative process, meaning that each time you search, you will come up with patents that will provide another level of keywords to search on. As you refine your search you should come up with all the similar patents and comprehensively cover the field.

First you want to decide on the scope of your search. What problem does your invention solve? This is a good place to start your search. You can use individual words or link words with Boolean operators like "and" or "or" to refine your search.

You can search keywords in a number of the text fields in the patents:

- Title of Invention (TTL)
- Abstract (ABST)
- Specification (SPEC)
- Claims (ACLM)

There are two databases: one of existing patents and one of published patent applications. Patent applications are published approximately 18 months after they are filed. A patent takes 2-3 years to be granted. You need to also examine the published applications to see if anyone has beaten you to the idea.

A number of patents will pop up in the search results and a quick initial review of the Titles of the Invention will give you an idea of which ones are relevant to review.

As you review the relevant patents you should also check their Classification. The USPC, IPC, and CPC codes will be listed. You should do searches of the classification codes that are relevant to see what patents pop up.

This process gets successively more granular and detailed and will provide you with the prior patents that have been awarded and the applications currently being reviewed in you invention's space.

This is your due diligence so be as thorough as you can as it is in your best interest to come up with good relevant references. You should come up with approximately 6-10 solid references.

Make sure you do your patent search on the USPTO website as commercial search engines sell the results of searches and you don't want anyone poaching your invention and ideas.

You also want to look for public domain prior art and search what might have been published in trade journals, literature, and commercial websites. You will need to use a commercial search engine like Google to do this research.

Evaluating the References

Look at what is disclosed in the Specifications and Claims and decide what you can claim that is novel and non-obvious. You may have to redraft some of your initial ideas about your invention based on what you find.

Summary of the Invention

Patent Rule 37 CFR 1.73 covers this next section Summary of the Invention. The Summary should follow closely the material laid out in the Claims section (we will talk about that section soon). Start with a summary of the independent claims which are the most significant part of the claims section. Then include the objects of the present invention. The objects essentially answer the question: why did you invent this? Draft one paragraph for each object or reason for the invention.

You also want to address all of the deficiencies and solve all the problems that you found in the prior art that you cited and investigated when doing your patent search due diligence.

Remember, one aspect of this application is that it is a sales document. You need to show how your invention is new, useful, not obvious, and novel to someone skilled in the art, meaning someone familiar with this field. You need to convince the patent examiner of this so make your argument clear and describe all the novel attributes of your invention and the problems they solve.

Brief Description of the Drawings

Patent Rule 37 CFR 1.74 details the requirements of the Description of the Drawings section. Describe the view of each Figure in the drawings usually in one sentence and start each Figure as a new numbered paragraph like this:

[0015] Fig 1 is a perspective view of ...

[0016] Fig 2 is a side section view of ...

[0017] Fig 3 is a flow diagram of....

The drawings detail the elements outlined in the Claims section. A good rule is to check that every noun mentioned in the Claims is represented on the drawings. The drawings must contain every feature described in the Claims.

The function of the drawings is to convey the concept; they are not drawn to scale and there are no dimensions or measurements included.

Detailed Description of the Invention

Patent Rule 37 CFR 1.71 discusses the requirements of the Detailed Description of the Invention section. The description and narrative in the detailed description of the invention must be coordinated with the Drawings and make sure to reference the drawings.

You also want to make sure that all the elements described in the Claims section are mentioned in the Detailed Description. Once you have completed the Claims sections, go back and confirm that every aspect of the Claims is represented in this Description section.

One strategy is to write the Claims first and use that as the basis for the Detailed Description.

Start this section by defining any terms that may help understand the nature of the invention. You want to make sure that the words you use are defined specifically as you want them to be understood.

The test to see if you are clear and detailed enough is: can someone of ordinary skill in this art with just this description and Drawings make and use this invention.

This is where the **Best Mode** of the invention is disclosed and discussed.

Claims

As per 35 USC 112:

- The claim or claims must particularly point out and distinctly claim the subject matter which you regard as your invention

- The claims define the scope of the protection of the patent

- Claims must start on a new page

- All claims must be one sentence long. You separate elements in the sentence with semi colons, and the last element with an "and".

- Make sure every word in the claims is included in the Detailed Description and discussed there.

- **Keep the claims clear and concise. Don't have superfluous claims. If someone can make the invention by leaving one element out, they don't infringe on your patent.**

Drafting the Claims

There are two types of claims: independent and dependent. Under the basic filing fee you are allowed up to 20 total claims, 3 of which can be independent. Independent claims are generally broad and cover a large part of the invention. Many times the independent claims can be structured as a "process" claims and one as a "machine" claim. This can cover the two aspects of the invention: how it does what is does (the method), and how it is made (the apparatus). Dependent claims refer to the independent claim and further narrow and restrict the broad nature of the independent claim.

Claim language can be thought of as either broad, or narrow and specific. Each claim must be one complete sentence and only one sentence

Each independent claim must be a workable portion of the invention and must not refer to any other claim

Each dependent claim must refer to one independent claim by a number smaller than the number of the depending claim you are writing. Dependent claims add features to the independent claim it refers to.

The structure of a claim is:

- Preamble: a method, or an apparatus…
- Transition: use the word: "comprising
- Body: this is where you describe the particular element

Use the present or future tense in writing the claims.

The sweet spot of number of claims is the minimum number of elements in order to support patentability. Too few render the claims incomplete and any superfluous ones make you vulnerable to someone being able to make the invention without infringing.

Don't get stuck on the formalities of this section. A good way to go about writing claims is to just start writing. The goal is to end up with a description of the invention that is complete and describes what you have pictured in your mind's eye.

As you need to add elements to the invention to define it more specifically, check to see if the pieces and parts being added have been introduced properly. These are your dependent claims.

Remember this is the place for full discloser of the invention; no trade secrets. Don't hide or mislead.

Abstract

The Abstract is the last section before the drawings. It must start on a new page and the page is left unnumbered.

The Abstract page must not exceed 150 words and should fairly describe the scope of the invention. It should be quite similar to your first Claim.

When you review patents on the USPTO website for the prior art section and due diligence, you will be reading, copying and responding to a number of patent abstracts. This review and practice should give you a good sense of how to craft your Abstract.

Patent Drawings

If you have a clear understanding of your invention it should not be a problem for you to create your own patent drawings. I suggest using Microsoft Word or Apple Pages. Whatever word processor you have used to draft the document will have adequate drawing tools for creating your patent drawings.

First, sketch out your drawing conception free hand with a pen or pencil. Then using the lines and shapes tools in your word processor translate the drawing into a document. There are some YouTube videos that can help you here but a little trial and error should get you up the learning curve pretty quickly.

Sample Patent Application Template

Here is where we apply all the rules we went over in Part II and incorporate them into the patent application format where you will describe your invention. This is the form of the document you will file with the USPTO.

TITLE OF INVENTION (keep this to six or less words)

STATEMENT REGARDING FEDERALLY SPONSORED R&D

This section most likely will not be applicable but if it is, follow the instructions on the USPTO website.

NAMES OF PARTIES TO A JOINT RESEARCH AGREEMENT

This section most likely will not be applicable but if it is, follow the instructions on the USPTO website.

CROSS REFERENCE TO RELATED APPLICATIONS

This section most likely will not be applicable but if it is, follow the instructions on the USPTO website.

Now we get into the generally applicable sections:

BACKGROUND OF THE INVENTION

1. Field of the Invention

[0001] The present invention is a system and methods for .... This section should be a short description of two sentences or so. It is used by the USPTO to figure out which examiner should review your application.

Each paragraph in your application is sequentially numbered in brackets.

2. Description of the Prior Art

[0002] U.S. Patent Number **X,XXX,XXX** relates to the use of.... This is where you detail the half dozen or so patents that are similarly related to your invention. Take the language from the patent's Abstract.

[0003] This patent does not teach the use of .... This next paragraph is where you describe all of the deficiencies and solve all the problems that you found in the cited patent. You need to clearly state what makes your invention unique and novel relative to the related ones you are citing.

[0004] U.S. Patent Number **X,XXX,XXX** relates to.... Repeat the process detailed above.

[0005] This patent does not teach the use of .... Repeat the process detailed above. Remember each paragraph is sequentially numbered in brackets.

SUMMARY OF THE INVENTION

[0016] The present invention is a system and methods for ... Organize this section as a summary of the independent Claims and aspects of the invention that line up with the deficiencies you described of the prior art.

[0017] Benefits of the current invention include: .... Here you can list all the benefits of your invention relative to the problems it solves.

[0018] It is therefore a primary object of the present invention to provide highly effective and accurate…..

[0019] It is another object of the present invention to identify and create, …..

[0021] It is another object of the present invention to attach …..

[0022] It is another object of the present invention to implement ….

[0025] It is another object of the present invention to create an embodiment of the invention for use with ....

[0029] It is another object of the present invention to create processes ....

You get the idea. You should be very thorough in listing the objects of your invention, the reasons why you invented it.

[0030] These and other objects of the present invention will become apparent to those skilled in this art upon reading the accompanying description, drawings, and claims set forth herein.

BRIEF DESCRIPTION OF THE DRAWINGS

[0032] Fig. 1 is a systems diagram detailing the best mode of the various sub systems of the present invention. The figure shows the …..

[0033] Figure 2 illustrates the process of ….

DETAILED DESCRIPTION OF THE INVENTION

1. Definitions

[0033] Here is where you define any terms that may have various meanings so that it is clear how you are using specific terms.

2. Best Mode of the Invention

[0034] The best mode of the invention as shown in Figures 1 and 2 is a system and methods for the application of ...

3. How to Make the Invention

[0035] The present invention is a system and methods for ....

Here is where you write out the details of how to make the invention and how to use it.

Benefits

[0036] Benefits of the current invention include: ....

Here you describe the benefits again.

CLAIMS

(Claims start on a new page)

What is claimed is:

1. A System for creating…. This is an independent claim. Independent claim sentences start with "A". An independent claim must be some workable portion of the invention.

2. The system according to Claim 1 wherein …. This is a dependent claim. Dependent claim sentences start with "The" and reference the independent claim they are associated with.

3. The system according to Claim 1, wherein …. This is another dependent claim. You get up to 20 claims under the basic patent fee.

4. A method for creating …. Here is another independent claim. This is a "method" claim where number 1 was a "system" claim. These are also referred to as "machine" and "process" claims.

5. The method according to Claim 4 using… This is a dependent claim.

TITLE OF INVENTION (put your title here)

ABSTRACT

The Abstract is the last section before the drawings. It must start on a new page and the page is left unnumbered. The Abstract page must not exceed 150 words and should fairly describe the scope of the invention. When you review patents on the USPTO website for the prior art section and due diligence, you will be reading, copying and responding to a number of patent abstracts. This practice should give you a good sense of how to craft your Abstract.

Patent Drawing

Everything in the Claims should be shown on the drawings. Here is a sample patent drawing. You can find lots of examples of patent drawings attached to the patents on the USPTO website or by searching the phrase "patent drawings". Create your drawings using the draw tools in Microsoft Word.

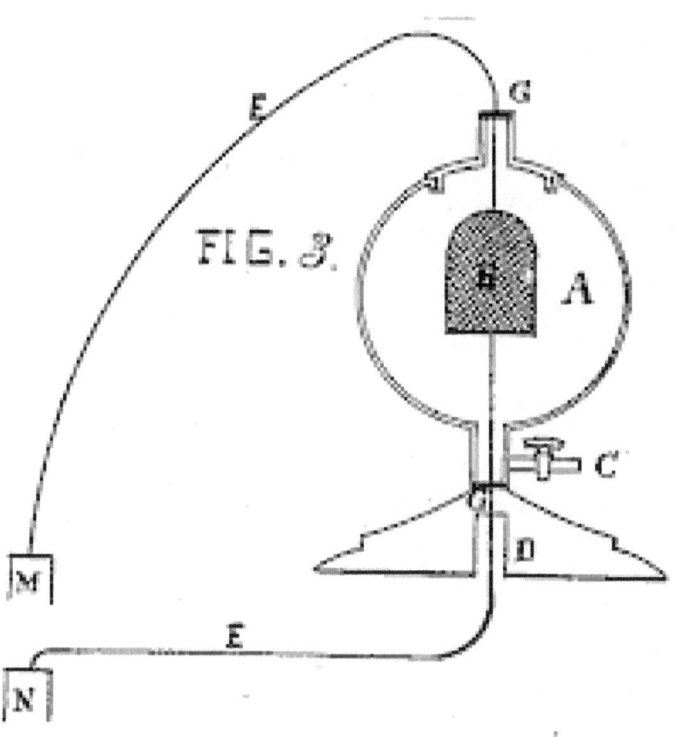

Congratulations! It's Time to File

Now that you have all the documents completed, its time to file your patent application. This is done through the USPTO Electronic Filing System (EFS) on their website www.uspto.org.

Create a PDF of your Word file. It should include:

- Application Data Sheet
- Certification of Micro Entity Status sheet
- Declaration (Oath of Inventorship)
- Information Disclosure Sheet: list all valid and relevant references including the ones you detail in the prior art section
- Your patent application document in the form and sequence we have discussed

Pay with a credit card.

As of this filing date you now can claim "Patent Pending" on your invention. Congratulations!

Patent Application Examination

Once you have filed your application with the USPTO it will be routed and examined by an appropriate staff examiner. There are approximately 8500 patent examiners with at least a Bachelor's Degree in the technological field they examine.

The work of examining patent applications for patents is divided among a number of examining technology centers (TCs), each TC has jurisdiction over certain assigned fields of technology. Each TC is headed by group directors and staffed by examiners and support staff.

The examiners review applications for patents and determine whether patents can be granted. The USPTO has over 12,000 employees, of whom about three quarters are examiners and others with technical and legal training. Patent applications are received at the rate of over 500,000 per year.

Examiner Process

Your examiner will review the contents of the application to determine if the application meets the requirements of 35 U.S.C. 111(a).

If the examiner does not think your application meets the requirements, the examiner will explain the reasons. The examiner will communicate with you through an Office

Action. This is the letter your will receive containing the results of their examination.

Some usual faults are:

- Missing items; here you need to supply what is missing.
- Objections to the form or structure requiring some re-write.
- Restriction Requirements: this is where it is determined that the patent application contains more than one independent invention. The claims are divided and you must elect what claims to patent from the choices given by the examiner. The non elected claims may be pursued separately in a Divisional Application.

There will also probably be rejections of some or all of the claims. These will fall into various categories such as: patentability, written description, or enablement. There may be 102 rejections based on Novelty.

Most likely the rejections will be of a 103 nature based on Obviousness. These are related to the scope and content of the prior art and that what you are proposing is a simple substitution or known technique, or predictable, or that it was taught, motivated, or suggested in the prior art.

It is your job here to demonstrate, by evidence or argument, why it is not obvious.

The best way to get a thorough idea of the examiner's reluctance is to have a phone call with the examiner. Representing yourself as a pro se applicant will allow you to have a forthright conversation with the examiner. Be respectful and not emotional and find out the specifics of the reasons for the rejection so you have the best opportunity to craft your response.

You will have opportunities to make amendments or argue against the examiner's objections.

If you fail to respond to the examiner's requisition within the required time, your application will be abandoned.

Amendment

Your Amendment document will begin with a Transmittal Sheet which is a cover sheet with a brief sentence stating that this correspondence and amendment is in response to a First Office Action (FOA).

This is followed by your amendments to the:

- Specification
- Claims

- Drawings

~~Cross out~~ deletions and <u>underline</u> additions.

Label your Claims as is appropriate:

- Original
- Currently amended
- New
- Canceled

Label your Drawings as appropriate in the top margin:

- Replacement Sheet
- New Sheet

Remember to change the Specification to reflect the Drawing changes.

Issuance Fees

When your patent is issued you will pay another fee of $240 for a Micro Entity. This makes your total patent fees for an issued patent $640 ($400 application plus the $240)

Summary

Now you have the information to draft, file, and amend your patent application. Use this book to reference the various steps and get started!

I hope you have found this book informative. This is powerful information that can have a great impact on your life and the life of others. Let me know if you have any comments or suggestions about the information or presentation provided here. Also let me know if you file an application and when it gets approved. My email is john.cousins@mba-asap.com.

I am rooting for you! Good luck!

For more great business related books check out

www.MBA-ASAP.com

Sign up for my Newsletter and get free books. Sign up at www.mba-asap.com and receive Reading and Understanding Financial Statements absolutely free.

Receive announcements of free and discounted books and courses.

About the Author

John is an author of over 20 books, blogger, podcaster, online course creator, investor, inventor, entrepreneur and musician. John began his career, after graduating from Boston University and MIT with degrees in Media Studies and Electronics, working for one of the great early Silicon Valley tech firms: Ampex. He then spent a decade in Manhattan working for ABC Television as a systems engineer designing and building facilities for the network and managing programs for sports and news; big spectacles like the Olympics and political conventions.

John then received his MBA from Wharton. He has since taken two companies public as CFO and CEO and has had 15 years experience as a public company CFO and ten years experience as a public company CEO. John has been involved in many start up and public company financings and deal making. He has founded numerous startups in alternative energy, life sciences, and technology. His career shifted to teaching at numerous universities in the U.S. and internationally in the past ten years. His company MBA ASAP delivers digital content on business topics via eBooks, paperbacks, audiobooks, podcasts and online courses. Visit http://www.mba-asap.com/

www.ingramcontent.com/pod-product-compliance
Lightning Source LLC
Chambersburg PA
CBHW020922180526
45163CB00007B/2851